D0391701

The Return of
Sherlock Holmes

SIR ARTHUR CONAN DOYLE

Level 3

Retold by Janet McAlpin
Series Editors: Andy Hopkins and Jocelyn Potter

Pearson Education Limited
Edinburgh Gate, Harlow,
Essex CM20 2JE, England
and Associated Companies throughout the world.

ISBN: 978-1-4058-5547-1

First published by Penguin Books 2000
This edition published 2008

1 3 5 7 9 10 8 6 4 2

Typeset by Graphicraft Ltd, Hong Kong
Set in 11/14pt Bembo
Printed in China
SWTC/01

Published by Pearson Education Ltd in association with
Penguin Books Ltd, both companies being subsidiaries of Pearson Plc

Acknowledgements:
Granada Television: pp. 2, 11, 20, 22–23
and 40–41; Scope Features: p. 35.

Every effort has been made to trace the copyright holders and we apologise in
advance for any unintentional omissions. We would be pleased to insert the
appropriate acknowledgement in any subsequent edition of this publication.

Contents

Introduction

'Sit down, Mr McFarlane,' said Holmes. 'No, I don't know your name. But I can see that you're an unmarried lawyer.'

The man seemed surprised at this, but it didn't surprise me.

'That's true, Mr Holmes,' he replied. 'And it's also true that I'm the unhappiest man in London today. Please help me! The police are coming to get me. I'm sure they followed me here.'

'The police are coming?' said Holmes. He looked very happy. I knew that he was hoping for an interesting case.

As a detective, Sherlock Holmes has a very clever mind. He also notices things that other people do not see. A person's clothes, hands, face or hair tell him a lot about that person, even before they speak. There are many examples of his skills in this book. In *The Six Napoleons* he soon realises that the busts, not Napoleon, are important. In *The Norwood Builder* he realises that one passage in the house is shorter than the passage below it. In *The Golden Glasses* he looks at a pair of glasses and immediately he is able to give a clear description of their owner.

When Sherlock Holmes has to solve an interesting case, his friend Dr Watson is usually at his side. Watson helps the great detective with his work, and makes notes. Later, he uses his notes to write the history of the case.

Dr Watson is not specially clever. In some of the films of the Sherlock Holmes stories he seems quite stupid, but he is an ordinary, sensible man and a good friend to the detective. He is also, of course, necessary to tell the story. Watson tries to understand how Holmes is thinking. This helps the reader to understand too. Watson is also a brave man. He is often able to help the detective in times of danger.

The writer of the Sherlock Holmes stories, Sir Arthur Conan Doyle, was, like Dr Watson, a doctor of medicine. He too stopped being a doctor when he discovered a more interesting activity.

Conan Doyle was born in Edinburgh, Scotland in 1859 and died from a heart attack at his home in south-east England in 1930. He studied medicine at Edinburgh University, and then in 1882 he started working as a doctor. While he was waiting for patients, he began to write. One of his teachers, Joseph Bell, was an unusually clever man. He noticed little things. He could often tell his patients about their jobs, their activities and perhaps their illnesses before they said a word. He taught his students that small pieces of information were important. When Conan Doyle began to write stories about his clever detective, he gave Holmes his teacher's skills. Sherlock Holmes is a quiet, cold man. He shows no interest in women and his only friend is Dr Watson. He is only interested in science and solving interesting crimes.

Conan Doyle's first story about Holmes, 'A Study in Scarlet', was printed in a magazine in 1887, and it was immediately popular. More stories followed, and after 1890 Conan Doyle became a full-time writer.

The short stories about Sherlock Holmes were printed first in Strand magazine. Later groups of stories came out in books like *The Adventures of Sherlock Holmes* (1892) and *The Memoirs of Sherlock Holmes* (1894). Conan Doyle also wrote four longer stories. The best known of these books is probably *The Hound of the Baskervilles* (1902). There have been many films and television programmes of this story.

The great detective became very popular. People wanted more and more of them. Many people thought that Sherlock Holmes was a real person. They wrote letters to him at 221B Baker Street and asked for his help. He was more well known than his writer, Conan Doyle. At last Conan Doyle decided to 'kill' his detective. He was tired of writing detective stories. He wanted to spend his time on more serious writing. He introduced into his Sherlock Holmes stories a very clever, scientific criminal, a 'Napoleon of Crime' called Professor Moriarty. Then, in 1893, Holmes followed Moriarty to Switzerland in a story called *The Final Problem*. The two men fought on a mountain top and both men fell to their deaths. Nobody saw the two men again. Holmes and his great enemy Moriarty were both dead. But this death was very unpopular with the readers, and with the magazine that printed these stories.

Everybody wanted more stories, so finally Conan Doyle had to bring Holmes back to life. These new stories were printed in a book called *The Return of Sherlock Holmes* (1904). You can read three of those stories here.

The world remembers Conan Doyle as the writer of Sherlock Holmes stories, but he wanted people to remember him for his more 'serious' writing – for stories from history, like *The White Company* (1890), *Rodney Stone* (1896) and *Sir Nigel* (1906).

Conan Doyle was also famous for other activities. He went as a doctor to help in the Boer War, and in 1902 he wrote a paper of great national interest, *The War in South Africa*. He worked to protect soldiers and sailors with better equipment. He tried to change bad laws. He also helped people who were wrongly punished for crimes.

In his later years he was more interested in studying ways of speaking with the dead. This was important work for him through his life and he wrote ten books on this subject. He believed that he had conversations with many famous men from history.

At the end of his life he was tired of hearing about his famous detective. 'Holmes is dead,' he said. 'I have finished with him!'

But today we remember him mostly for giving us Sherlock Holmes and Dr Watson. He made them real, and many visitors to London still look for their rooms in Baker Street. The building at 221 Baker Street is only business offices, but they have a special 'Sherlock Holmes room' there for lovers of Conan Doyle's stories.

A Note from Dr Watson

My friend Sherlock Holmes was one of the cleverest and most important detectives in England some years ago. The police often asked him to help them. My name is Dr Watson, and I helped Holmes with many of his cases. I kept careful notes and wrote about them.

In 1891, Holmes and I had to leave England on a very dangerous case. While we were away, Holmes disappeared. Everyone thought that he was dead. I was very sad at the news.

Then, one day in 1894, Holmes returned to England. He was not dead! At first this was a secret, because he was working on another case. But when the case was finished, we were able to work together again. Holmes was now a better detective than ever before.

This little book is called *The Return of Sherlock Holmes*. The stories come from my notes of the cases that we worked on after his return. Three of the best cases are here: *The Six Napoleons*, *The Norwood Builder* and *The Golden Glasses*. I hope you will enjoy reading them.

Dr Watson

Sherlock Holmes and Dr Watson outside their home in Baker Street.

The Six Napoleons

Mr Lestrade, a detective from Scotland Yard, often visited my friend Sherlock Holmes and me in the evening. Holmes enjoyed talking to Lestrade because he learned useful facts about Scotland Yard – London's most important police station. Lestrade liked these visits too, because Holmes was a good detective. Holmes always listened carefully if Lestrade had a difficult case. He often helped Lestrade.

On one of these evening visits, Lestrade talked about the weather and other uninteresting things for a long time. Then he stopped talking and sat quietly. Holmes was interested in his silence.

'Have you got a good case for me today?' he asked.

'Oh, nothing important, Mr Holmes,' said the detective.

Holmes laughed. 'Please tell me about it,' he said.

'Well, Mr Holmes, there is something, but it doesn't seem very important. I don't want to trouble you with it. I know you like difficult problems. But I think that this will perhaps interest Dr Watson more than you.'

I was surprised when Lestrade said this. I like helping Sherlock Holmes with his detective work, but I am really a doctor, not a detective. So I said, 'What's the matter? Is somebody ill?'

'Yes, I think so. I think that somebody is very ill,' was Lestrade's answer. 'I think that he is completely mad! Someone is stealing cheap busts of Napoleon Bonaparte and breaking them. I think he hates Napoleon. Four days ago, he went into a shop in Kennington Road. The owner's name is Morse Hudson and he sells pictures and other works of art. When the shop assistant was busy, the madman ran in. He picked up a bust of Napoleon, broke it into pieces and then ran away. Nobody saw his face.'

'Why are you so interested in this?' said Holmes.

'Because he's done it again,' replied Lestrade. 'Yesterday he got into the house of a doctor – Dr Barnicott. This doctor is very interested in Napoleon. He lives near Morse Hudson's shop, and he bought two busts there. He kept one bust at home and the other in his office, two miles away. The thief took the bust from his home and broke it against the garden wall. Dr Barnicott found it when he got up in the morning. He then went to his office – at about twelve o'clock. To his surprise, the second bust was broken too. The pieces were all over the room.'

'This is more interesting,' said Holmes. 'Now please tell me, were these three busts exactly the same?'

'Yes, they were.'

'Well,' said Holmes, 'why did the man choose these three busts? I'm sure that there are hundreds of other busts in London. I think the thief was only interested in the busts, not in Napoleon.'

'That's possible,' Lestrade replied, 'but can we be sure? There is no other shop that sells busts in that part of London. Perhaps the madman lives in that area and began with the nearest busts. What do you think, Dr Watson? Can someone hate Napoleon so much?'

'Yes, it's possible,' I said, and I told them some interesting examples from the history of medicine. 'But,' I said, 'how did this madman know where these three busts were?'

'It's very interesting,' said Sherlock Holmes. 'Please tell us, Mr Lestrade, if you learn more.'

◆

Next morning I was dressing when Holmes came into my room. 'Lestrade wants to see us immediately,' he said. 'He's at a house in Kensington.'

I quickly finished dressing. We had a cup of coffee, then we went to Kensington.

The house was in a quiet street, but it was not far from the busy centre of London. That morning there was a large crowd of people standing outside.

Lestrade was waiting for us. He was looking very serious. I noticed that there was a lot of blood outside the front door of the house.

Lestrade told us to come inside. There we met Horace Harker, the man who lived there. He worked for a newspaper, and today he had a good story. But he could not write about it; he was too frightened.

'Please tell us what you know, Mr Harker,' said Lestrade.

'I was woken by a loud cry at about three o'clock this morning,' he said. 'I was very frightened, but I went downstairs. There was nobody in the room, but the window was open and my bust of Napoleon was not there. So I opened the front door to call a policeman. I found a dead man lying there. He was covered in blood – I felt very sick.'

'Who is the dead man?' asked Holmes.

'We don't know,' Lestrade answered. 'He had a cheap street map of London and a photograph of a very ugly man in his pockets. There was a small knife near him. But I don't know if he was killed with that knife.'

'What about the bust of Napoleon?' asked Holmes.

'We found it quite near here, in the garden of an empty house,' said Lestrade. 'It was broken, like the others.'

Lestrade took us to look at the broken bust. Mr Harker stayed at home. He was beginning to feel better and he wanted to write the story for his newspaper.

◆

We soon arrived at the empty house. The pieces of the bust were lying in the grass by the garden wall. Holmes picked up some pieces and looked at them carefully.

'What do you think?' said Lestrade.

Holmes looked at him. 'There's a lot more work for us to do,' he said. 'But there are some interesting questions here that we must think about. For example, why did a man kill someone for a cheap bust like this? And if he only wanted to break the bust, why didn't he break it at Mr Harker's house? Why did he take it away with him?'

'Maybe he carried it away because he didn't want Mr Harker to hear him,' said Lestrade.

'Perhaps that's the reason,' said Holmes. 'But why did he bring it to this house and not another one?'

'Because this house was empty,' replied Lestrade.

'But there's another empty house in this road, nearer to Mr Harker's house. Why didn't he break it there?'

'I really don't know,' replied Lestrade.

Holmes pointed to the street light above our heads. 'He could see what he was doing here. The garden of the other house was too dark.'

'That's true!' said the detective. Then he asked, 'But how does this help us, Mr Holmes?'

'I don't know yet,' my friend answered, 'but I'm going to think about it. What are you going to do next, Mr Lestrade?'

'I want to find out who the dead man was. I need to know why he was in Kensington last night. Then I'll know who killed him outside Mr Harker's house. Isn't that a good idea?'

'Perhaps,' replied Sherlock Holmes. 'But it isn't my way.'

'So what are *you* going to do?' asked Lestrade.

'I'll do things in my way and you can do things in your way,' said Sherlock Holmes. 'Then we can talk about the case together later.'

Then he added something surprising. 'If you see Mr Harker, please tell him this. I'm sure that a dangerous, Napoleon-hating madman was in his house last night.'

Lestrade was surprised. 'Do you really think that's true?'

Holmes laughed. 'Not really,' he said, 'but I think the readers of Mr Harker's newspaper will be interested. We must go now, but please visit us in our rooms in Baker Street at six o'clock this evening. Until then, can I keep the photograph that the dead man had with him? After you come to Baker Street, you must come out somewhere with me. Goodbye and good luck!'

◆

Mr Harker's bust was from Harding Brothers' shop in the High Street, so Sherlock Holmes and I walked there together. Mr Harding was not there.

Holmes was not pleased by this. 'We'll come back in the afternoon,' he said to Mr Harding's assistant. 'And now, Watson, let's visit Mr Morse Hudson's shop. Dr Barnicott bought his busts there.'

Morse Hudson was very angry about the broken busts, but he answered all Holmes's questions. 'The busts were made by Gelder and Company, in another part of London,' he told us. 'I can't give you more help than that.' But when Holmes showed him the photograph from the dead man's pocket, he cried, 'That's Beppo!'

'Who's Beppo?' asked Holmes.

'He's an Italian. He worked in my shop for a time – a useful man – but he left last week. I don't know where he went. He left two days before the bust was broken.'

We thanked Morse Hudson and left his shop. Holmes was quite pleased with what the shopkeeper told us. He decided next to visit Gelder and Company, the factory where the busts were made.

We passed through many parts of London, rich places and poor places, before we came to Stepney. Stepney was a rich place in the past, but now poor working people lived there. Many of them came from other countries.

We soon found Gelder and Company. We spoke to a German. 'In the past we made hundreds of busts,' he told us, 'but this year we only made six. Three were sold to Morse Hudson and three to Harding. The busts were cheaply made, usually by Italian workers.'

When Holmes showed him the photograph of the ugly Italian, he became angry.

'That's a very bad man,' he said. 'His name is Beppo and he worked here for me. But that was more than a year ago.'

'Why did he leave?' Holmes asked.

'He tried to kill another Italian with a knife, in the street,' replied the German. 'The police followed him here and caught him. The other Italian didn't die, so Beppo was only sent to prison for a year. One of his friends works here now. Do you want to speak to him?'

'No, no!' said Holmes. 'Please don't tell him anything – this is very important.'

'All right,' the man said.

'I have one more question,' said Holmes. 'It says here, in your book, that you sold the busts on 3rd June last year. When did the police come for Beppo? Can you remember?'

'Yes, I can. I paid Beppo for the last time on 20th May last year, and it was very soon after that.'

'You've helped me a lot,' said Holmes. 'I must go now. Remember, don't say anything to Beppo's friend.'

It was late in the afternoon and we were hungry. So we stopped to have some food in a restaurant. Holmes bought a newspaper. In it was an exciting story by Mr Harker about the madman who hated Napoleon. Most of the story was not true, but Holmes laughed a lot. He thought that it was a good joke.

'This is very helpful, Watson,' he said.

I did not really understand what he meant. But I laughed too at the silly story.

After our meal, we went to Harding Brothers. Mr Harding was a busy little man, and he answered our questions quickly and clearly. His three busts were all sold: one to Mr Harker of Kensington, one to a Mr Josiah Brown of Chiswick, and the third to a Mr Sandeford. Mr Sandeford lived outside London, in Reading.

Holmes seemed very interested in these facts and thanked Mr Harding. It was late, so we hurried back to Baker Street. We had to meet Lestrade.

◆

Lestrade was waiting for us when we arrived. He was very pleased with himself.

'Have you found out anything, Mr Holmes?' he asked.

'Well, we know a lot about the busts now,' replied Holmes.

'The busts!' said Lestrade, and laughed. 'I know you're a clever detective, Mr Holmes. But I think I've found out something more important than that!'

'What have you discovered?'

'I now know who the dead man was. And I think I've found the motive for his murder,' was Lestrade's reply.

'Very good, Mr Lestrade.' Holmes smiled and waited.

Lestrade continued. 'We have a detective at Scotland Yard who knows many of the Italians in London. He knew this man well. His name was Pietro Venucci – a thief and a very dangerous man. Venucci worked for the Mafia. He punished people who broke the rules of the Mafia. That was his job. Usually he killed them. I think the man in the photograph broke the rules. Venucci was following him. They had a fight and Venucci was killed.'

Holmes smiled and said, 'Very good, Mr Lestrade, very good. But I still don't understand why the busts were broken.'

Lestrade almost shouted at Holmes, 'Those busts aren't important! Can't you forget them, Mr Holmes? A man will only go to prison for six months for breaking busts. Pietro Venucci is dead. That's what interests me.'

'I see,' said Holmes quietly. 'What are you going to do next, Mr Lestrade?'

'I'm going to go to the area of London where the Italians live. I want to find the man in the photograph. Do you want to come with me?'

Holmes did not seem very interested. 'No, thank you. I think that we can find him more easily in another place tonight.'

'Really! Where?'

'At an address in Chiswick. If you come with me tonight, I will go with you tomorrow,' said Holmes.

Lestrade was surprised, but he agreed. The three of us had an early dinner together. Then Holmes told Lestrade and me to rest until eleven o'clock.

Holmes did not rest. He spent the time in his room looking at some old newspapers. He was, I thought, probably looking for some facts about Venucci or Beppo.

◆

Lestrade and I woke up at half past ten. Holmes was waiting for us. He told me to bring my gun. I noticed that he took his favourite strong walking stick with him.

We quickly drove to Chiswick, and Holmes took us to a large house in a dark street. The house, too, was dark and quiet. The people inside were probably already asleep in bed.

'I'm glad that it's not raining,' said Holmes quietly. 'It's possible that we'll have to wait a long time. We mustn't smoke and we must be very quiet. I hope we're going to discover something tonight.'

We only had to wait for five minutes. The garden gate suddenly opened, and a man ran quickly down the garden path towards the house.

We could not see his face. It was too dark and he was moving too quickly. He disappeared into the darkness and we waited in silence.

Next, we heard the sound of a window opening very slowly.

10

'I hope we're going to discover something tonight.'

Then we saw a small light inside the front room of the house.

'Let's go to the open window. Then we can catch him as he comes out,' said Lestrade.

But before we moved, the man came outside again. He was carrying something. He looked around him. He saw that nobody was watching him. Then there was a sudden crash as he broke the thing against the wall.

We ran forward. Holmes jumped on his back and the man fell heavily to the ground. Lestrade and I quickly went to help Holmes. I had my gun ready. Soon the man was our prisoner.

He looked up at us. His face was very ugly. We could see that he was surprised and angry. I realized immediately that he was the man in the photograph.

While we were holding the man on the ground, Holmes was looking at the broken pieces of another bust of Napoleon. He lifted up each piece and looked at it in the light.

11

Somebody turned on the lights in the house. Then a short fat man in a shirt and trousers came out towards Holmes.

'You're Mr Sherlock Holmes, aren't you?' he asked, with a smile on his face.

'That's correct,' said Holmes. 'And you are Mr Josiah Brown.'

'Yes, sir. We did what you told us. We locked the doors to the house and turned off the lights. Then we waited very quietly. You've done very well. Please come inside and have some food and drink.'

Holmes thanked Mr Brown, but Lestrade wanted to take the man away. So we all drove to Scotland Yard. The thief said nothing, but he looked at us all the time. His ugly white face was like an animal's.

When we arrived at Scotland Yard, the man was searched. He had nothing with him except a long knife with dry blood on it and a little money.

As we were leaving, Lestrade said, 'Well, Mr Holmes, I must thank you for all your help. My ideas were correct – don't you agree?'

Holmes smiled and said, 'It's a little late at night now for me to explain. But I think the business of the busts is very important. It's much more important than you think. Can you come and see me again at six o'clock tomorrow evening?'

'Of course,' said Lestrade. 'I'm always happy to visit you. I'll be pleased to come.'

As we were going home, Holmes said to me, 'Lestrade is a good detective, but he doesn't understand everything about this case. I think this is a very unusual case, Watson.'

'Really?' I said. 'Is there more to explain?'

'The busts, Watson. I think they're the most important part of this case.'

◆

At six o'clock the next evening, Lestrade came to Baker Street to see us. He now knew more about Beppo. The Italian was a well-known thief. He spent time in prison after he knifed a man. We already knew that. Beppo was, Lestrade said, very good at making busts and other works of art. It was possible that Beppo made the busts of Napoleon at Gelder and Company.

Holmes listened to Lestrade's words with a smile on his face. But I could see that he really wanted to tell Lestrade something. I was sure that it was something very surprising.

There was a knock on the door and the servant brought an old man into the room. He had a red face and he was carrying a large bag. He put the bag on the table.

'Is Mr Sherlock Holmes here?' he asked.

Holmes smiled and said, 'I'm Sherlock Holmes. And I think that you're Mr Sandeford of Reading. I'm pleased to meet you. This is my friend Dr Watson, and this is Mr Lestrade from Scotland Yard.'

We both said hello to Mr Sandeford.

'I have the bust of Napoleon for you,' he told Holmes.

He also had a letter. 'Mr Holmes sent me this letter yesterday,' he said to Lestrade and me. He read it to us.

Dear Mr Sandeford,

I know from Mr Harding that you bought the last bust of Napoleon in his shop. I want that bust very much and I will pay ten pounds for it. Please bring it to my rooms in Baker Street, London, tomorrow at half past six.

Sherlock Holmes

Then he said to Holmes, 'Do you know how much I paid for the bust in this bag?'

'No, I don't,' said Holmes.

'Well, I'm not a thief, Mr Holmes. You should know that I only paid one pound for it. If you don't want to buy it now, I'll understand.'

'No,' said Holmes. 'I still want the bust. Here's ten pounds.' He gave the money to Mr Sandeford.

'Thank you very much,' said Mr Sandeford.

He took the money and opened the bag. Inside was an ordinary white bust of Napoleon, just like the others.

Holmes said, 'Thank you, Mr Sandeford. Now, before you go, I want you to sign this piece of paper. It says that you've sold the bust to me for ten pounds.'

'Of course,' said Mr Sandeford. He signed the note and left.

Holmes watched Mr Sandeford leave. Then he took a clean white cloth from a cupboard and put it on the table. Lestrade and I watched him carefully. He put the bust carefully on the cloth. Then he took his stick and hit the bust hard. It broke into small pieces.

Holmes shouted with excitement and picked up something small and black from the cloth. Lestrade and I were silent.

'This is the Black Pearl of the Borgias!' said Holmes.

We were both very surprised.

'Really, Holmes?' I cried, 'How did you know that it was there?'

'It's impossible,' said Lestrade quietly.

Holmes explained. 'This is the most famous pearl in the world. It was stolen from the hotel room of the Princess of Colonna on 22nd May last year. I'm sure that you remember that, Mr Lestrade?'

'Yes, I do,' replied Lestrade.

'Well,' Holmes continued, 'you will also remember where the hotel was. The princess was staying in the same part of London as Gelder and Company. The police thought that the thief was an Italian servant in the hotel, Lucretia Venucci. But they never proved it. I think that her brother, Pietro, was killed two nights ago.

'When I looked at my old newspapers, I discovered

something. Beppo was caught only two days after the pearl was stolen. The busts were made in those two days. Perhaps the Venuccis stole the pearl from the hotel, and Beppo stole it from them. I don't know exactly, but it doesn't matter.

'I am sure now that Beppo had the pearl with him on the night of his street fight. He ran away, and the police followed him. Beppo ran to Gelder's and wanted to hide the pearl – but where? He didn't have much time. He saw the new white busts of Napoleon drying on the table. They were still soft, so he pushed the pearl into one of them. Then he covered the hole. It was the perfect place to hide the pearl.

'Because of the street fight, Beppo was sent to prison for a year. During that time, the six busts were sold. But we know that Beppo's friend still worked at Gelder's. I think that Beppo asked him to find the names of the buyers of the busts. So when Beppo came out of prison, he started looking for the bust with the pearl in it.

'He got a job with Morse Hudson. There, he learned where the first three busts were. Then he left the job, returned and broke the first bust. Next, he broke Dr Barnicott's busts. But he didn't find what he was looking for. The other three busts were sold to Mr Harding's shop. Beppo found out who had them. I'm not sure how he did that. Perhaps an Italian friend was working there.

'At the same time, Venucci knew that Beppo was out of prison. He wanted to find him. He was sure that Beppo knew the pearl's hiding place. Venucci was following Beppo when he went to Mr Harker's house in Kensington. They fought, and Beppo killed Venucci.'

'But,' I asked, 'if Venucci knew Beppo well, why did he carry his photograph?'

'To show to other people,' replied Holmes. 'Of course,' he continued, 'I wasn't sure that Beppo didn't find the pearl in Mr Harker's bust. But if he didn't, there were only two more busts. One was in Chiswick and the other one was in Reading.

Chiswick is much nearer than Reading, so I told Josiah Brown and his family to be ready.

'We were lucky. Beppo went to Mr Brown's house first, and we caught him. I knew then that the pearl was in Mr Sandeford's bust.

'Mr Harker's newspaper report helped us. His story made Beppo very happy. The police seemed to have the wrong idea – they were looking for a Napoleon-hating madman. He didn't think that anyone knew the true secret of the busts. But when I heard the name Venucci, I immediately thought of the missing Black Pearl.'

'Mr Holmes,' said Lestrade, 'I've seen your work on many cases in the past, but this is one of the best. I'm sure that my friends at Scotland Yard will be very interested in the case. They will also be interested in the way that you've solved it. Can you come and meet them tomorrow? They will be very pleased to talk to you.'

'I shall be happy to come,' said Holmes. 'Thank you.'

'Thank *you*, Mr Holmes,' said Lestrade. 'You've helped me to understand this case, and you've found the famous Black Pearl for me.'

Holmes smiled at the police detective. He didn't know what to say. Then suddenly his face changed.

'Well, Watson,' he said, 'we have to do some work now. This is not our only case! Goodbye, Lestrade. If you have any more little cases for me, please tell me. I'll be happy to help you if I can.'

The Norwood Builder

'There seem to be no interesting cases these days, Watson,' Sherlock Holmes said to me. 'London isn't a very interesting place.'

'I don't think the people of London will agree with you,' I answered.

He smiled as he pushed his chair back from the breakfast table. 'You're right – I mustn't be selfish,' he said. 'It is better for everybody if detectives like me have little work.'

I smiled too. The world did seem very quiet that morning.

Sherlock Holmes sat back in his chair, picked up his newspaper and started reading. Suddenly, there was a loud knock on the front door.

I heard the servant open the door. Then somebody ran into the house and up the stairs. He opened our door and stood in front of us. He looked very frightened.

'I'm sorry, Mr Holmes,' he cried. 'I must talk to you now. I can't wait. I'm John Hector McFarlane. I'm sure that you know my name.'

'Sit down, Mr McFarlane,' said Holmes. 'No, I don't know your name. But I can see that you're an unmarried lawyer.'

The man seemed surprised at this, but it didn't surprise me. Holmes was a good detective, and even I noticed the man's untidy clothes and the lawyers' papers in his hand.

'That's true, Mr Holmes,' he replied. 'And it's also true that I'm the unhappiest man in London today. Please help me! The police are coming to get me. I'm sure that they followed me here. I'll go with them if you'll help me.'

'The police are coming?' said Holmes. He looked very happy. I knew that he was hoping for an interesting case. Then he remembered poor Mr McFarlane and said, 'I'm sorry,

Mr McFarlane. This seems very interesting. Please tell me more. Why are the police looking for you?'

'They think I killed a man. His name's Jonas Oldacre.'

The newspaper was still lying on the table, and our visitor picked it up. I noticed that his hands were shaking.

'Look at your newspaper,' he said. 'You'll see why I've come to you, Mr Holmes,' he said. 'Look at this.'

FIRE IN LOWER NORWOOD. RICH MAN DISAPPEARS. IS HE DEAD? WAS HE KILLED?

I took the newspaper and looked at the report. The police, it said, wanted to find Mr McFarlane.

'They think I killed Mr Oldacre for his money,' said the poor man. 'What will my mother think? What can I do?'

I looked at Mr McFarlane carefully. He was a handsome man with fair hair, and he was probably about twenty-seven years old. His clothes showed that he had plenty of money. Then I looked at Sherlock Holmes. His eyes were closed, so I read him the newspaper report.

Late last night, or early this morning, there was a fire in Sydenham Road in Lower Norwood. The police are worried about Mr Jonas Oldacre, the owner of the house.

Mr Oldacre is well known in the area. He made a lot of money as a builder, but has stopped doing building work. He is sixty-two years old, unmarried and lives at Deep Dene House. He has few friends.

Mr Oldacre still keeps a lot of old wood at the back of his house. When a fire started there last night, at about twelve o'clock, the wood burned fast.

At first, it seemed like an ordinary fire. But then someone noticed that the owner of the house was not

18

there. In one room there were some important papers on the table and signs of a fight. A stick was found on the floor and also some blood.

Mr Oldacre had a visitor last night, a lawyer called John Hector McFarlane. The police think that the stick belongs to him.

There are also signs that something heavy was pulled through the grass, from the house to the fire. Something – an animal or a person – was burned with the old wood. The police think that Mr Oldacre was killed in his house. Then he was taken outside and burned. They are looking for Mr McFarlane. Mr Lestrade, of Scotland Yard, is working on the case.

When I finished reading, Sherlock Holmes opened his eyes. 'So why, Mr McFarlane, haven't they found you yet?' he asked.

'I live with my mother and father at Torrington Lodge, in Blackheath,' said Mr McFarlane. 'But last night I wasn't at home. I stayed at a hotel in Norwood because my visit to Mr Oldacre finished very late. The police will try to catch me today. I think they'll come here for me.'

Suddenly there was another knock on the front door, and we heard policemen's voices. Two men waited outside and one joined us upstairs. It was our friend Lestrade, the detective from Scotland Yard.

Lestrade looked straight at McFarlane and said, 'John Hector McFarlane, you must come with me. We believe that you killed Jonas Oldacre last night.'

McFarlane stood up. His face was white.

'Sit down,' said Holmes. 'And Mr Lestrade, please sit down too.'

'But I must take Mr McFarlane away,' said Lestrade.

'Half an hour won't matter to you,' replied Holmes. 'And Mr McFarlane wants to tell us what happened last night.'

'Mr McFarlane wants to tell us what happened last night.'

'Well, Mr Holmes,' said Lestrade. 'Because you're my good friend, I'll wait for half an hour – but no more.'

'Thank you,' said Holmes. Then he asked Mr McFarlane to tell us his story.

Mr McFarlane began. 'Yesterday morning I knew nothing about Mr Oldacre except his name. He was a friend of my mother and father a long time ago, but not now. I was very surprised when he came to my office yesterday.

'I'm a lawyer. Mr Oldacre showed me some papers – his will – which I have here. He asked me to make a good copy of the will. He wanted to wait, so I began the work. I soon saw, to my surprise, that he wanted to give me all his money after his death. I asked him why he wanted to do that. He explained. He had no children, but he knew my father. So he wanted me to have the money.

'Of course, I thanked him for his great kindness, but I was still very surprised. I made the copy as quickly as possible. Finally, it was finished. He asked me to go to his house that evening to see some more important papers. His last words to me were, "Please don't tell your mother and father. I want this to be a surprise for them."

'Mr Oldacre was being very kind to me. I wanted to do exactly what he said. So I sent a message to my parents. I had important business after work, I said. I told them not to worry if I did not come home.

'Mr Oldacre asked me to be at his house at nine o'clock, but I couldn't find it. I didn't arrive until half past nine. Mr Oldacre—'

'Stop!' said Holmes. 'Who opened the front door?'

'An old woman. I think she worked for Mr Oldacre.'

'And did she know your name?'

'Yes,' replied the young lawyer. 'Then she took me into a room. There was a simple meal waiting for me on the table. I ate some of the food and then Mr Oldacre came and took me to another room. He had a lot of papers in a cupboard there, and we worked on these together for a long time. We didn't finish until about half past eleven. Mr Oldacre told me to leave quietly by the back door because the old woman was asleep.

'When I was leaving, I couldn't find my stick. But Mr Oldacre said, "That doesn't matter, my boy. You can get it another day. I hope you're going to visit me very often."

'When I left him, the cupboard was open. The papers were still on the table. I couldn't go back to Blackheath – it was too late. So I stayed at the Anerley Arms in Norwood. I didn't know about all this until I read the paper this morning.'

Mr McFarlane stopped speaking and Lestrade said, 'Have you any more questions, Mr Holmes?'

'No. I want to go to Blackheath first,' said Holmes.

'Don't you mean Norwood?' asked Lestrade.

'Perhaps I do,' replied Holmes, and he smiled at Lestrade.

'We didn't finish until about half past eleven.'

Holmes often understood things more quickly than Lestrade, and the police detective knew this.

Lestrade turned to Mr McFarlane and said, 'There are two policemen waiting for you outside. You must go with them now.'

The policemen took Mr McFarlane away. His face was still white and he looked at us sadly, but he said nothing.

◆

Lestrade stayed in the room with us after McFarlane left. Holmes picked up the lawyer's papers and looked at them. Then he passed them to Lestrade.

'These are very interesting, aren't they?' he said.

Lestrade looked at the papers for a minute, then said, 'I can understand the first few lines perfectly; the writing is good. After that, the writing is very bad and I can't read it. Later, there are some more good lines, then the writing is bad again.'

'Why do you think it's like that?' asked Holmes.

'Why do *you* think it's like that?' replied Lestrade.

'The answer is very simple,' said Holmes. 'Mr Oldacre wrote this on the train, on his way to London. The good parts were written at stations. The bad parts were written when the train was moving.'

Lestrade laughed and said, 'Very good, Mr Holmes. But how does that help us with the case?'

'Well,' said Holmes, 'most people don't write their wills on trains. It seems that this will wasn't really very important to Mr Oldacre.'

'It *was* very important,' said Lestrade. 'His will is the reason that he's dead now.'

'Do you think that's true?' asked Holmes.

'Don't you?' replied Lestrade.

'It's possible, but the case isn't very clear to me yet.'

'Not clear?' said Lestrade. 'It's very clear to me. When

McFarlane knew about Mr Oldacre's will, he went to Norwood. He killed Mr Oldacre, and then he burned the dead body. It seems very simple to me.'

'Too simple,' said Holmes. 'McFarlane is not stupid. A clever man doesn't kill a man on the same day that he made his will. And the man's servant knew that McFarlane was in the house. Does a clever man carefully burn the body, and then carelessly leave his stick in the house?'

'You know very well, Mr Holmes,' said Lestrade, 'that a murderer doesn't always think very clearly just after his crime. It's easy to forget something like a stick. Perhaps he was afraid to go back into the house. What other motive is there for Mr Oldacre's murder?'

'I can think of many possible motives,' said Holmes. 'Here's an example. A thief was passing the house and saw the two men in a room with the papers. He thought that they had money there. When one of the men left, the thief came in through the window. Then he killed the other man.'

'Why didn't he take anything?' asked Lestrade.

'Because he found only papers; there was no money in the room,' said Holmes.

Lestrade did not seem very sure of his ideas now, but he said, 'Well, you can look for your thief if you want to, Mr Holmes. But I think that McFarlane was Mr Oldacre's killer. He had a motive. He was also the only person in the world who did not need to take anything from Mr Oldacre's house. It was already his, in Mr Oldacre's will.'

'I didn't say that you were wrong,' replied Sherlock Holmes. 'I only wanted to show you that there were other possible motives for Mr Oldacre's death. And now, goodbye Mr Lestrade. I will probably see you at Norwood later today.'

Lestrade left us, and Holmes put on his coat.

'I'm going to Blackheath,' he said.

'Why not Norwood?' I asked.

'Two strange things have happened, my friend, and the police are only thinking about one of them. The first thing was the strange will. Why did Oldacre want to give his money to Mr McFarlane? I'm going to find out.'

'Do you want me to come with you?' I asked.

'No, it isn't necessary; you can't help me. There's no danger at Blackheath,' replied Holmes.

CD 2   ◆

It was quite late when my friend returned from Blackheath. He was not happy.

'I'm afraid that the case is difficult, Watson,' he said. 'This time I think that perhaps Lestrade is right. I still don't think that McFarlane killed Oldacre. But the facts are helpful to Lestrade and they don't help me. I'm afraid that he'll win.'

'Did you go to Blackheath?' I asked.

'Yes, I did,' said Holmes. 'And I quickly discovered that Oldacre was a very unpleasant man. I spoke to Mr McFarlane's mother. She was very angry and afraid. Oldacre wanted to marry her many years ago. She agreed, but later she changed her mind. She heard that he was unkind to his animals.

'This made Oldacre angry. On the day of her marriage to Mr McFarlane, he destroyed her photograph and sent the pieces to her with a letter full of hate. If the police discover this, they'll think badly of young Mr McFarlane. He clearly had another possible motive for killing Oldacre.'

After meeting Mrs McFarlane, Holmes then went to Norwood. He showed me the simple plan of Oldacre's house and garden which he made there. The garden was large, and the fire was a long way from the nearest road. Lestrade was not there when Holmes arrived. But another policeman showed him everything.

'They've found some pieces of Oldacre's clothes where the

fire was,' continued Holmes, 'and some burnt parts of an animal or a person. I looked at everything very carefully but I found nothing new. There's very little blood inside, and there are only two men's footprints on the floor.

'I looked at the papers on the table. Some of them were in packets, closed with red wax. Mr Oldacre's bank book was there too. I was surprised to see the amount of money in it. He had less money in the bank than people believed. It was not enough to make McFarlane rich!

'Then I spoke to the old woman, Oldacre's servant. I think she knows something. But she told me very little. She let McFarlane into the house at about half-past nine and soon went to bed. She didn't wake up until people started shouting about the fire. She thinks that the burnt pieces of cloth come from Mr Oldacre's clothes that night. That's what she told me. But I'm sure that she's hiding something. I can feel it.'

Next, Holmes told me a strange thing. Oldacre was paying money to a 'Mr Cornelius'. This was one reason why he had very little money in the bank. Nobody knew who Cornelius was.

Holmes then became very serious. 'I'm afraid that Lestrade will be able to hang Mr McFarlane for murder,' he said. 'And I don't know how to stop him.'

I went to bed soon after this. But I do not think that Holmes slept all night.

◆

When I got up next morning, Sherlock Holmes was reading the morning newspapers. There was a letter from Lestrade on the table. It said:

Come to Norwood soon. I have discovered a new fact. I am sure now that McFarlane killed Oldacre – Lestrade

'Lestrade is clearly very pleased that he's right. He thinks that I'm wrong for the first time,' said Holmes. 'I must go to Norwood. Please, Watson, will you come with me? I need a friend today.'

We drove together to Oldacre's house. Lestrade was waiting for us there.

'Hello, Mr Holmes,' he cried. 'Have you found your thief yet?'

'I haven't found anything yet,' replied Holmes.

'Well, I have,' said Lestrade.

'You do seem very pleased with yourself,' Holmes answered.

Lestrade laughed loudly. 'Sherlock Holmes doesn't like being wrong, does he, Dr Watson?' he said to me. I did not reply and he continued, 'Please come this way.'

He took us into the house.

'McFarlane came this way after he killed Oldacre,' he said. 'Now look at this.'

He pointed to a mark on the wall. It was a thumbprint and it was the colour of blood.

'That's John Hector McFarlane's thumbprint,' said Lestrade. 'It's exactly the same as the print which McFarlane made in prison this morning.'

He showed us a piece of paper with McFarlane's thumbprint on it.

'That's the end of the case,' said Lestrade proudly.

'Yes, it is,' I agreed.

'Yes, it is,' said Holmes in a strange voice. I looked at him and was surprised. He seemed very happy. Lestrade continued to talk proudly, but Holmes was quietly laughing at him.

'Very good!' said Holmes. 'This is a lesson to us all.'

'Yes, it is,' the detective replied.

'Who discovered this thumbprint?' asked Holmes.

'Mr Oldacre's servant, the old woman. She found it this morning,' said Lestrade.

'Are you sure that the mark was there yesterday?' said Holmes.

Lestrade thought that my friend was mad. I did not understand what his question meant either.

'Mr Holmes,' said Lestrade, 'how do you think that McFarlane got out of prison? And if he did get out, why did he come here?'

Then Holmes said, 'Well, it's his thumbprint, we can be sure of that.'

'Yes, we can,' said Lestrade. 'And now I must go. I'm a busy man and I must write my report on this case.'

He went quickly into the sitting room and closed the door.

'Why were you so pleased about the thumbprint?' I asked Holmes.

'Because I know that it wasn't there yesterday. I looked at that wall very carefully. The police didn't look as carefully as I did. That's why they're not the best detectives. Now, Watson, let's go for a walk in the garden.'

I followed Holmes. I couldn't understand how the thumbprint got there. And I could see that Holmes did not want to tell me yet. He looked at every part of the outside of the house. Then we went back inside and he looked carefully in every room. We looked in every cupboard and walked down every passage.

We were in the last passage, at the top of the house, when Holmes suddenly started laughing.

'This is an interesting case, Watson,' he said. 'Lestrade thinks that he's better than me. He had fun when we were talking about the thumbprint downstairs. But I think that I can have some fun now. What shall I do . . .? I know!'

We went down to the sitting room where Lestrade was working.

'Are you writing your report, Mr Lestrade?' Holmes asked.

'Of course I am,' the detective replied.

'Isn't it too early for a report?' Holmes asked.

Lestrade put down his pen and looked at him. He knew Holmes well. He could see that he had important news.

'What do you mean?' he asked.

'Well, there's one important person in this case that you haven't spoken to,' said Holmes.

'Really? Who? Can you show me this person?' said Lestrade.

'Yes, I think I can,' said Holmes, 'but I shall need some help. How many policemen are there here?'

'Three,' said Lestrade.

'Are they strong men, with loud voices?' asked Holmes.

'Yes, they are. But how can their voices help us?'

'You'll soon find out,' said Holmes. 'Now, please ask one policeman to bring a few old newspapers. There are some in the kitchen. The other two must bring plenty of water.'

The policemen brought the things, and all six of us went up to the top of the house. The policemen were smiling. Lestrade still thought that Holmes was mad. I did not know what my friend wanted to do.

Sherlock Holmes walked to the end of the passage and carefully put the newspapers on the floor. Then he said, 'Watson, please open the window, and then start a fire here.'

I did what he asked. The papers soon started to burn. Next Holmes said, 'Now I want you all to shout, "Fire!" with me. Shout as loudly as you can. One, two, three—'

'Fire!' we all shouted.

'Again!' cried Holmes.

'FIRE!'

'Again!'

'FIRE!' we shouted as loudly as possible.

Suddenly the wall at the end of the passage opened, like a door. An ugly little man ran out, like a rabbit coming out of its hole.

'Very good,' said Holmes. 'Watson, put some water on the fire, please.' Then he said, 'This is Mr Jonas Oldacre.'

'Where have you been for the last two days?' said Lestrade, in a strange voice.

Oldacre laughed, but he was clearly afraid of Lestrade. 'I haven't hurt anyone,' he said.

'You haven't hurt anyone!' repeated Lestrade angrily. 'Because of you, Mr John Hector McFarlane is in prison. We thought that he killed you. He was almost hanged by the neck for murder!'

'I only did it for a joke,' said Oldacre.

'You aren't going to play any more jokes now!' said Lestrade. He told the policemen to take Oldacre away.

When they left, Lestrade said, 'I must thank you, Mr Holmes. I was rude to you earlier today and I'm sorry. I really thought that the case was finished. Mr McFarlane mustn't die for a crime that he didn't do!'

'Don't worry,' said Holmes kindly. 'Nobody will know what happened. You can change your report. It isn't necessary to say that I helped.'

'But don't you want people to know about your skills?' asked Lestrade.

'No,' said Holmes. 'I'm happy with my work, and that's enough for me. Now, let's see where that rabbit was living.'

The end of the passage was closed to make a small room. Inside it there was a little furniture. On the table there was some food and water and some papers. When the door was shut, it was impossible to see the room behind it.

'Oldacre was a builder. He was easily able to make this place for himself,' said Holmes. 'He only needed his servant's help with his plan.'

'How did you know that he was here?' asked Lestrade.

'I thought that he was hiding somewhere in the house,' Holmes replied. 'I saw that this passage was shorter than the one below it. Then I realized where he was.'

'That was clever,' said Lestrade. 'But why did you think that he was in the house?'

'The thumbprint,' said Holmes. 'It wasn't there yesterday

when I looked. So somebody put it there last night.'

'But McFarlane was in prison. How was it done?'

'When Oldacre and McFarlane were working on the papers, they used a lot of red wax. They used it to close the packets,' said Holmes. 'Oldacre asked McFarlane to do that job because he wanted a clear thumbprint in the soft wax. Later, Oldacre used the same wax to put McFarlane's print on the wall. He probably used blood from his own thumb.'

'Wonderful!' said Lestrade. 'Wonderful! But why did he do all these things, Mr Holmes?'

I wanted to laugh. This proud detective was asking questions like a child with his teacher.

'That doesn't seem difficult,' said Sherlock Holmes. 'Oldacre hated McFarlane's mother. A long time ago, she refused to marry him. You didn't know that, Lestrade, because you never visited Blackheath.

'Oldacre is a very unpleasant and dangerous man. He waited many years to make Mrs McFarlane unhappy. Then at last he thought of a way to plan her son's death. The law hangs her son for murder, and at the same time he makes some money for himself.'

'Makes some money? How?' asked Lestrade.

'His papers show that Oldacre had money problems,' said Holmes. 'He wanted to disappear without paying his bills. He paid a lot of money to a "Mr Cornelius". But I don't think that Mr Cornelius exists. Oldacre planned to change his name to Cornelius after he disappeared.

'The will gave Mr McFarlane a motive for murder. And the fire explained why there was no dead body. It was a clever plan. Mr Cornelius could come alive in another part of England after Mr Oldacre died in Norwood. But now, Mr Lestrade, let's go and ask him some more questions.'

We went down to the room where the policemen were

keeping Jonas Oldacre. When he saw us, he said again, 'I only did it for a joke. I didn't want to hurt dear Mr McFarlane.'

'I don't think that anyone will believe that,' said Lestrade. 'I think you'll have to go to prison, Mr Oldacre.'

'And I think the police will take all Mr Cornelius's money too,' Holmes added.

Oldacre looked at Holmes and said in a very angry voice, 'I'll kill you, Sherlock Holmes!'

Holmes smiled and said, 'You're not the first man who has said that to me. But you'll be too busy in prison for the next few years. Before you go, I have a question for you. You burned something like a dead body with the wood. What was it? Was it a dead dog, or perhaps some rabbits?'

Oldacre sat in angry silence. Holmes laughed and said, 'He doesn't want to tell us, Watson. Well, it isn't important. If you ever write the story of the Norwood builder, put "rabbits".'

The Golden Glasses

Sherlock Holmes and I worked on many cases in 1894, but this was one of the most interesting.

It was a very stormy night near the end of November. Sherlock Holmes and I were reading by the fire. It was late, and most people were already in bed.

Holmes put down his book and said, 'I'm glad that we don't have to go out tonight, Watson.'

'I am too,' I replied.

Then, above the sound of the wind and the rain, I heard something outside the house. I went to the window and looked out into the darkness.

'Someone is coming here,' I said.

'Who can it be, at this hour?' Holmes answered.

We soon learned who our visitor was. It was Stanley Hopkins, a young detective from Scotland Yard. Holmes and I were sometimes able to help him with his cases.

'Sit down by the fire,' said Holmes. 'It's so cold and wet tonight. Have you got an interesting case for me?'

'Yes, I have,' the detective replied. 'Have you seen the newspapers this evening, Mr Holmes?'

'No,' said Holmes. 'I've been busy with a book.'

'It doesn't matter,' Hopkins said. 'There were only a few facts in the papers. The case is very new – the police at Yoxley only sent for me this afternoon.'

'Where is Yoxley?' I asked.

'It's in Kent,' he replied. 'It's a very small place. I thought it was going to be an easy case. Now it seems very difficult. A man is dead. But I really don't know why anyone wanted to kill him.'

'Tell me everything,' said Sherlock Holmes.

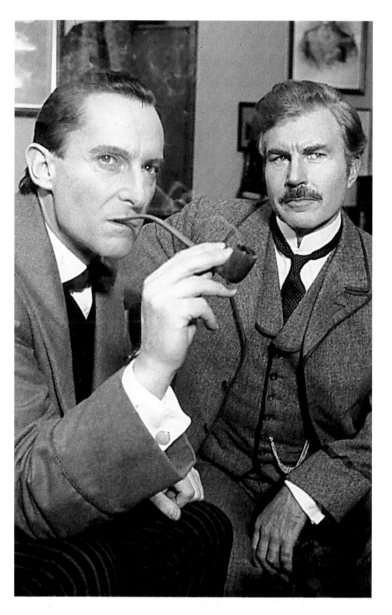

'Tell me everything,' said Sherlock Holmes.

'Yoxley Old Place is a large house in the country, near a small village,' said the detective. 'About ten years ago an old man, Professor Coram, came to live there. He was ill, and walked with a stick. After a few months, his neighbours became friendly with him, but they didn't often visit his house. They say he's very clever. He spends most of his time working with his books. He has a gardener, Mortimer, and two servants. The cook is Mrs Marker and the other servant is Susan Tarleton. They're good servants, and they've been with him for a long time.

'The professor is writing a book. About a year ago, he decided to employ a secretary. A man came, but he wasn't very good and he didn't stay very long. A second man came. He was called Smith. He became a good friend and helper to the professor. They worked together every day, and the book's nearly finished. But now the young man is dead. And I think someone killed him.

'As I said before, very few people visit the house. The people in the house don't go out very often either. Old Mortimer lives in a little house in the garden.

'Yoxley Old Place is near the London road. A visitor can easily go through the garden gate to the house, get in and escape quite quickly.

'I spoke to Susan Tarleton, the servant girl. She was working in one of the bedrooms between eleven and twelve o'clock this morning. Professor Coram was still in bed; he often gets up late. Smith was in his bedroom, reading a book. After a few minutes she heard him go down to the professor's study. Suddenly she heard a very loud cry. She ran down to the room. She found Mr Smith lying on the floor. He was nearly dead. There was blood on his neck, and a lot more on the floor.

'Mr Smith said a few words in a weak voice before he died. Susan Tarleton thinks he said, "The professor – it was she."

'I spoke to the cook next. She arrived in the room after Mr Smith died. The two women quickly went to the professor's bedroom. He was still in bed. He, too, heard the loud cry, but he can't get out of bed without help. Mortimer has to help him get up at twelve o'clock every day.

'I spoke to the professor. He can't think of any reason why Mr Smith was killed.

'Mortimer got the police, and they sent for me. When I arrived, I told everyone not to walk on the garden path. Nothing in the house was moved either.

'I think that someone very clever came to the house this morning. There were no footprints on the garden path. But I saw signs that someone walked along the grass near the path. That person didn't want anyone to know about his or her visit to the house.

'I went to the study and looked at Mr Smith's body. There was a small knife on the floor. I think he was killed with that. It's the professor's, and he always kept it on the table in that room. And we found these.'

He gave Holmes a pair of glasses. Holmes took them and looked at them very carefully. After a few minutes, he took a piece of paper and wrote something on it. Then he gave it to Stanley Hopkins. Hopkins read the note.

'Look for a woman who has plenty of money. She wears good clothes, has a thick nose, and her eyes are close together. She looks closely at things. She has probably visited an optician more than twice during the last two months. Her glasses are unusually strong, and quite expensive. There are not many good opticians in London, so you can find her name easily.'

The detective was surprised when he read this. I was too. Holmes looked at our faces and laughed.

'Glasses can tell us many things about the people who wear them,' he said. 'These glasses belong to a woman — they're very pretty. Mr Smith said "it was she" before he died. That, too, tells me that a woman was there. She has money and likes good things. Why? Because the glasses are made of gold. And they're made for a thick nose, and eyes that are close together.'

'But how did you know that she looks closely at things? And about her visits to the optician?' I asked.

Holmes replied, 'These glasses are very strong, so the woman has very weak eyes. People with very weak eyes always look closely at things to see them better. And the optician? It's clear that the glasses were mended twice, at different times. Can you see here? The gold is very new and yellow. Here it's a little older.'

Hopkins said, 'You're always so clever, Mr Holmes. You know more about this case than I do now. And you've never been to Yoxley Old Place! Will you and Dr Watson come there with me tomorrow?'

We both said yes. We had to catch the train at six o'clock next morning. So Holmes asked Stanley Hopkins to stay with us for the night.

◆

The next day the weather was better, but it was still very cold. We took the train to a small town near Chatham. We had breakfast there before we continued to Yoxley Old Place.

A policeman was waiting for us at the garden gate. Stanley Hopkins asked him some questions, but there was no new information.

Hopkins said to Holmes, 'Here's the garden path, Mr Holmes. You can see that there are no footprints on it.'

'Which side were the prints on the grass?' asked Holmes.

'Here,' said Hopkins, pointing to one side of the path.

'The grass is very narrow here,' said Holmes. 'Yes, I can see that someone has walked on it. Is this the only way to get from the road to the house?'

'Yes,' said the detective. 'I'm sure that it is.'

'So did the lady come back this way too?'

'Yes, I think so.'

'That was very clever of her,' said Holmes. 'She needed to walk very carefully, as she has weak eyes. Well, I've seen everything that I want to see in the garden. Let's go into the house. The door to the garden is always open, so she could get in easily,' Holmes continued. 'I don't think she planned to kill anyone. She didn't bring a knife or a gun. She used the professor's knife from the table.'

We went into the house and Holmes said, 'She came down this passage, but she didn't make any footprints on the floor. Then she came into this room. How long was she here? Do you know?'

'She was only here for a few minutes, Mr Holmes,' replied Hopkins. 'The cook cleaned in here only a quarter of an hour before Mr Smith was killed.'

'Good,' Holmes said. 'So she wasn't here for more than fifteen minutes. She went to that cupboard by the table. It's the only piece of furniture in here with a lock on it. If there's anything important in the room, it's in there.'

He went down on his knees and looked at the door of the cupboard. Then he stood up, and said, 'Look!' He pointed at the door. 'There's a small mark near the keyhole. Why didn't you tell me about this, Hopkins?'

'I didn't think it was important,' said the detective. 'There are always marks by keyholes.'

'I know,' said Holmes. 'But this mark is very new. I think it was only made yesterday. Is Mrs Marker here?'

'Yes,' said Hopkins. 'I'll call her.'

A sad-faced woman of about fifty came into the room. She was Professor Coram's cook. She also helped to clean his house.

Sherlock Holmes asked her to look at the mark by the keyhole. 'Tell me, Mrs Marker,' he said, 'did you see this mark when you cleaned the room yesterday?'

'No, sir, I didn't.'

We took the train to a small town near Chatham.

'I'm sure that you didn't,' said Holmes. 'I think that Mr Smith's killer made it. Who has the key to this lock, Mrs Marker?'

'The professor has it,' she replied. 'He keeps it in his room with him.'

Holmes's next question was, 'Is it an ordinary key?'

'No, sir,' she replied. 'That's a very strong lock. It's a special kind of key.'

Holmes thanked Mrs Marker, and she left the room. Then he said to us, 'Now we know what happened. The lady came into this room. She went to the cupboard, and tried to open it. Smith came in while she was doing that. She quickly tried to take the key out of the lock. She made that mark because she was in a hurry. Smith went to her, and she picked up the knife. He held her. As she tried to get free, she dropped her glasses. He was too strong for her, so she used the knife. He fell to the floor, and she ran out of the room without her glasses.

'There are two passages outside. One goes to the back door. The other goes to the professor's room, doesn't it?'

'Yes,' said Hopkins. 'There's no way out of the house along the second passage.'

'Let's go and see the professor now,' said Holmes.

We went down the passage to the professor's room.

Holmes looked at the walls and floor of the passage, and said, 'What do you notice about this passage that's strange?'

'Nothing,' said Stanley Hopkins. 'It is just like the other one.'

'That's what I mean,' said Holmes. 'The walls and floor are exactly the same colours as in the other passage.'

'Is that important?' asked the detective.

'Possibly,' replied Holmes. 'But I am not sure about that yet.'

We went into the professor's room. It was a very large room, and the walls were covered with books. There were too many books, so some of them were lying on the floor in front of the shelves. The professor's bed was in the middle of the room, and the professor was lying in it. He had white hair and a big white beard, but the beard was dirty and yellow near his mouth. He was smoking a cigarette. Like his beard, his hand was yellow from cigarettes. The room smelt strongly of cigarette smoke. There were boxes of cigarettes everywhere.

The professor said, 'Do you smoke, Mr Holmes? These are very good cigarettes; I smoke a lot of them. I'm happy when I'm smoking. I can't walk easily, so I can't go out. I only have my work and my cigarettes. Now Smith is dead and I can't even work. He was a good young man; he helped me a lot. I'm sorry about what has happened to him – very sorry.'

Holmes took a cigarette and lit it. He walked round the room while he smoked it. The professor continued talking.

'I'm happy that you've come, Mr Holmes. I'm sure that you'll be able to help us.'

I noticed that Holmes was smoking more quickly than usual. He smoked four cigarettes while the professor talked.

The professor told us about his work – he was writing a history of Egypt.

'I'm old now,' he said. 'My work is my only happiness. My work and my cigarettes. I can see that you like them, too, Mr Holmes. They're very special cigarettes. They're sent to me from Egypt. I smoke too much, I know. But sir, you smoke even faster than I do!'

At last the professor stopped talking.

Holmes then said, 'You were in bed when Smith was killed. So I know that you don't know anything. But can you tell me what his last words meant? "The professor – it was she."'

'No, I can't,' said the professor. 'But Susan Tarleton is only a girl. Perhaps she didn't listen carefully. I'm sure that he wasn't speaking clearly. Remember, he was dying!'

'Can you think of any reason for his death?' was Holmes's next question.

'Well, Mr Holmes,' said the professor. 'I'll say this only to you, because it's not very nice. I think he killed himself. I think he was in love. He had some glasses that belonged to a woman. Perhaps he loved her very much, but she didn't love him. People sometimes kill themselves for that reason.'

Holmes looked surprised at that idea. He thought deeply about it. He walked up and down the room silently. At last he spoke to the professor again.

'What's in the cupboard in the room where Smith died?' he asked.

'Nothing for a thief, Mr Holmes,' the professor replied. 'Just papers and letters from my poor wife. She's dead now. You can look in the cupboard if you want to. Here's the key.'

Holmes took the key and looked at it. Then he said, 'No, I don't think I need to look in the cupboard. Perhaps you're right about Smith, Professor Coram. I'll think about your idea. Perhaps I'll have an answer for you after lunch. I'll come to you again after two o'clock. I'm sure that you need to rest.'

The professor looked pleased when Holmes said this. He said, 'Yes, I am tired. I want to be alone now. Please don't come here until two o'clock.'

Holmes and I walked in the garden. Holmes didn't seem very happy or interested in the case. I asked him, 'Do you think that you can find the answer now?'

'I'm not sure,' he replied. 'But I'm interested in the cigarettes that I smoked.'

'Really? Why?'

'You'll see later,' he said. 'Now, here comes Mrs Marker. I'll talk to her again for five minutes.'

He began talking to the cook. 'You probably don't cook much for the professor, do you?' he asked. 'Smokers like him don't usually eat much.'

'Sometimes he eats a lot, sometimes only a little,' she said.

'And today?' Holmes asked. 'I saw him smoke a lot of cigarettes. I'm sure that he didn't want any breakfast today.'

'You're wrong, sir!' the cook replied. 'He had a large breakfast, and then he asked for a large lunch. I was surprised. When I heard about poor Mr Smith's death, I didn't want to eat anything. The professor's a strange man.'

After this, Holmes did not talk very much. He listened to Susan, the servant, without asking questions. She told him about Mr Smith's visit to the village on the morning before his death.

At two o'clock, Holmes said to the young detective, 'Now we must go and see the professor again.'

◆

The old man's lunch was finished. The food was gone, and his plate was clean. He was sitting on a chair, and he was already smoking another cigarette.

'Well, Mr Holmes,' he said. 'Have you solved this case?'

He pushed his box of cigarettes towards Holmes. Holmes put out his hand to take one. But he knocked the box off the table, and the cigarettes fell on the floor.

Holmes got down on the floor and picked them up. Then he stood up and said to Professor Coram, 'Yes, I've solved it!'

'Really?' said Professor Coram. 'Where did you find the answer? In the garden?' His face was angry as he spoke to Holmes.

'No,' said my friend. 'The answer is here in your bedroom!'

'And when did you find this answer?'

'Two minutes ago,' said Holmes.

Then the professor said, 'You're not being serious, Mr Holmes. This is an important case – Smith is dead. Please don't joke about it.'

'I'm not joking,' said Holmes. 'I am sure about what I know. I don't know everything yet. But I know that you've done something bad. I'll tell you what I think.

'Yesterday, a lady came into your house and went into your study. She had a key to the cupboard. It was a new key, with a sharp point, and it made a mark near the lock. There's no sharp point on your key, Professor. I noticed that when you gave it to me this morning. She didn't use your key. And you didn't know that she was in the house. She came here, as a thief, to steal something from the cupboard.'

'This is all very interesting,' said Coram. 'But can't you tell us more? What happened to this lady after that?'

'I'll try to tell you,' replied Holmes. 'Your secretary came into the room and found her there, and she killed him. I think his death was a mistake. She didn't plan to kill anybody. I know that because she didn't bring her own knife.

'She lost her glasses in the fight, but she had to run away quickly. Her eyes were not good and she made a second mistake. She went down the wrong passage. It was an easy mistake, because both passages have floors and walls of the same colour. She didn't go to the outside door – she came to your room, Professor.'

'Do you mean that she came in here? She came in here and I didn't even see her?' cried the professor. His face was white.

'No, I don't mean that. She came in here and you did see her!' said Holmes. 'I think you knew her. You spoke to her and helped her.'

The professor laughed loudly. 'You're mad, Mr Holmes, mad! Where is this woman now?'

Holmes pointed at one of the walls. 'She's there, behind the bookshelves!' he said.

We all looked at the shelves that he was pointing to. We could only see books. Then the shelves began to move. The wall was opening like a door. The professor cried out loudly as a woman came into the room.

'Yes,' she said in a strange voice. 'I'm here!'

'You must come with me,' Hopkins said to her.

'I will not try to escape,' the woman replied. 'You know that I killed Smith. I have not got very much time, but I want to tell you about this man.'

She pointed at the professor. 'He is not English – he is Russian. I will not tell you his name, because that is not important.'

Professor Coram seemed a little happier when she said this. He replied, 'Thank you, Anna, thank you.'

She looked at him angrily. 'Why do you want to live?' she asked him. 'Your life is nothing – you are an animal!'

She turned to us again. 'I am this man's wife,' she continued. 'We lived in a city in Russia. I will not tell you the name of that city.'

Again the old man said, 'Thank you, Anna.'

'We were revolutionaries,' she said. 'We were fighting to make our country a better place. We had friends who were also revolutionaries. The police wanted to catch us and send us to prison – or kill us.

'We decided to kill a policeman. We wanted to show people that we were strong. One day one of us did kill a policeman. The police could not catch us, so they offered a lot of money for the name of the killer.

'My husband told the police the name of the killer. He got the money. All the other revolutionaries were caught. Some of us were killed, and some of us were sent to prison. I was lucky; I was only sent to prison for ten years.

'One young revolutionary, Alexis, did not want us to kill the policeman. He tried to stop us. He wrote letters to me about it. But my husband hid those letters because he wanted Alexis to die. Alexis was lucky – he did not die. But he went to prison for a very long time. He is in prison now, and he will stay there for another twenty years.'

She looked at the professor very angrily and said, 'Yes, he is in prison, and you are free. You animal!'

The woman's face was white. She looked weak and ill. 'I must finish what I am saying quickly,' she said. 'I came out of prison last year. I wanted to get the letters that Alexis wrote to me. If the government in Russia sees them, they will know about Alexis. They will know that he tried to stop the killing of the policeman. Then they will let him out of prison.

'I came to England to find my husband. I did not know where he was living. I spent a long time finding Yoxley Old Place. When I found his new home, I sent a man here. He was the first secretary, the man who worked here before Smith. He found out where the letters were kept. He got a key for me. But then my husband asked him to leave.

'So I had to come here. When I was coming to the house, I met Mr Smith. I did not know that he worked for my husband. I asked him the way to Professor Coram's house.'

'Yes,' said Holmes. 'I think he told the professor about your conversation. That's why he said, "The professor — it was she." It was a message for Professor Coram about you. The killer was the woman that he spoke to that morning.'

'I must have your permission to speak,' said the woman. Her face was even whiter than before. 'I did not want to kill Smith. I used the knife because it was the only thing on the table. It was the first thing that I saw. I ran out of the room, but I lost my glasses. I could not see. I came down the wrong passage, into this room.

'My husband was frightened and angry when he saw me. He wanted to call the police. But I knew that he could not do that. He did not want other revolutionaries to know his address. I wanted to escape because of Alexis. And my husband wanted me to escape because he was afraid of my friends.

'He decided to hide me from the police. There is a secret place behind the bookshelves. Only he knew about it. I stayed there for many hours. He took large meals and gave me food. He talked to me about leaving. When the police left, I could go. He promised to say nothing.'

The woman took a small packet from her dress and gave it to Holmes. 'I must finish,' she said strangely. 'These are my last words. Here is the packet of letters that will save Alexis. Take it! You are a good man. You will make sure that it gets to the Russian Embassy in London. There is nothing more ...'

'Stop her!' cried Holmes. As she fell to the floor, he jumped to her side. He took a small bottle from her hand.

'Too late,' she said. 'Too late! I took the poison before I left my hiding place. Please, sir, remember the packet!'

◆

Soon we were able to catch the train back to London. Holmes said to us as we were travelling, 'That wasn't really a difficult case, but the glasses were important. I couldn't solve the case without them. It was clear to me that the woman's eyes were very weak. So when she lost her glasses, she couldn't see well.

'There were no marks on the path, and she couldn't run straight along the grass without her glasses. It's too narrow. So I knew that she never left the house.

'It was her first visit to the house, and she made a mistake. The two passages are nearly the same, and she went down the wrong one. There's no door from the professor's room to the garden.

'I thought that perhaps she was still in the professor's room. But where?

'I looked at the floor. It was very strong. I didn't think that there were any secret places under it. Then I looked at the bookshelves. You can often find a secret place behind them in old houses. There were books all over the floor except in one place. Maybe there was a secret door there, I thought.

'I smoked a lot of cigarettes, knocking the ash on the floor in that place. When the woman came out for food, her feet made marks in the ash. Then I was sure that the woman was there.'

Our train was now arriving in London.

ACTIVITIES

A note from Dr Watson and The Six Napoleons (pages 1–10)

Before you read

1 Discuss these questions.

   a What do you know about Sherlock Holmes and Dr Watson? Have you seen films or television programmes of Sherlock Holmes stories? Have you got a favourite story?

   b Who was Napoleon? When did he live, and in which country was he born?

2 Look at the Introduction.

   a What do you learn about Dr Watson?

   b Why did Holmes have to die in *The Final Problem*?

3 Look at the Word List at the back of the book.

   a Talk with another student. What are the words in your language? Check the meanings of new words in your dictionary.

   b Which four of these words are words for people's jobs?

4 The first story is called 'The Six Napoleons'. What do you think the six Napoleons are? (The answer is in the Word List.)

While you read

5 Which is the right word?

   a Lestrade has an *important/unusual* case.

   b When Lestrade first talks to Holmes, somebody has broken *three/four* busts of Napoleon.

   c The next day the case becomes *more/less* serious.

   d The dead man has a *knife/photograph* in his pocket.

   e Beppo worked for Gelder and Company until a *week/year* ago.

   f *Lestrade/Holmes* thinks the busts are not important.

After you read

6 Which of the men in the story are described below?

a He sold two busts from his shop in Kennington Road.

b He sold three busts from his shop in the High Street.

c He bought busts for his home and his office.

d A man is murdered outside his house.

e He worked for Gelder and Company and Mr Hudson.

7 Who says these words, and why are they important?

a 'But I think this will perhaps interest Dr Watson more than you.'

b 'Now please tell me, were these busts exactly the same?'

c 'I'll do things in my way and you can do things in your way.'

d 'He's an Italian. He worked in my shop for a time – a useful man.'

e 'Those busts aren't important! Can't you forget them?'

The Six Napoleons (pages 10–16)

Before you read

8 Someone has stolen and broken busts of Napoleon that were made by Gelder and Company. Discuss these questions.

a Where are the other busts?

b Who do you think killed Pietro Venucci, and why?

c Why is Holmes going to go to Chiswick now?

d Why are the busts so important to someone?

While you read

9 Who:

a do Holmes and his friends catch in Chiswick? ....

b owns the fifth bust? ....

c brings the sixth bust to Holmes? ....

d knows that the pearl is the famous Black Pearl? ....

e owned the pearl? ....

f hid the pearl in a bust? ....

g knew that Beppo had the pearl? ....

h is very happy with Holmes's work? ....

After you read

10 What happens first? Number the sentences, 1–6.

    a Beppo kills Venucci.   .....

    b Mr Sandeford sells a bust of Napoleon to Holmes
       for £10.   .....

    c A thief steals the Black Pearl of the Borgias from
       the Princess of Colonna.   .....

    d Holmes, Watson and Lestrade catch a man outside
       a house in Chiswick.   .....

    e Holmes breaks the bust and finds the black pearl in it.   .....

    f Beppo hides the pearl in one of the six busts at Gelders.   .....

11 How do these people feel? Give reasons for your opinions.

    a Holmes, about Lestrade

    b Lestrade, about Holmes

    c Holmes, about Watson

    d Watson, about Holmes

12 Imagine that you are Mr Sandeford. You receive a letter from Holmes. He wants to buy your bust of Napoleon for £10. You take the bust to his house. When you go home, you talk to your wife. Tell her what happened there. How do you feel?

13 What does Lestrade want Holmes to do at the end of the story? Why?

The Norwood Builder (pages 17–26)

Before you read

14 Discuss these questions.

    a In this story, a man comes to Holmes for help. The police are sure that he is a murderer. What do you think? Why?

    b In those days in Britain murderers were hanged. Now they go to prison for a long time. What happens to murderers in your country?

    c Where can you find footprints and fingerprints? Why are they important to the police?

15 Are these sentences right (✓) or wrong (✗)?

    a The police think Mr McFarlane killed Mr Oldacre.   .....

    b Mr Oldacre is, or was, a rich man.   .....

    c Mr Oldacre's dead body was found behind his house.   .....

    d When Lestrade arrives, he immediately takes Mr McFarlane to Scotland Yard.   .....

    e Mr Oldacre leaves all his money to Mr McFarlane in his will.   .....

    f Mr Mcfarlane spent last night at his parents' house.   .....

    g After Lestrade leaves, Holmes goes to Norwood.   .....

After you read

16 Work with another student. Have this conversation.

    Student A: You are Mr McFarlane. Tell Holmes what you did yesterday. Start from Mr Oldacre's arrival at your office.

    Student B: You are Holmes. Ask questions. Make sure that Mr McFarlane's story is clear to you.

17 Discuss these questions.

    a Why is Lestrade sure that McFarlane killed Oldacre?

    b What does he think happened?

    c What reasons does McFarlane have for murdering Mr Oldacre?

The Norwood Builder (pages 26–33)

Before you read

18 Discuss these questions.

    a Is Mr Oldacre really dead? If not, where is he?

    b Why did Mr Oldacre want to leave his money to Mr McFarlane?

19 Complete these sentences with one word.

    a Mr Oldacre wanted to .... McFarlane's mother.

    b Lestrade finds a red .... on the wall.

    c Holmes asks Watson to start a .... in the passage at the top of the house.

    d Mr Oldacre says he only hid for a ....

    e The passage upstairs was .... than the passage downstairs.

    f Oldacre was able to make his secret room because he was a ....

    g Oldacre planned to change his name to ....

After you read

20 Why are these important to the story?

    a the handwriting of Mr Oldacre's will

    b the fire behind Oldacre's house

    c the thumbprint on the wall in the house

21 Imagine that you are Mr Oldacre, after the end of the story. You are at the police station with Lestrade. Tell him everything that you did. Tell him why.

22 How does Lestrade change his feelings and opinions from the beginning to the end of the case?

The Golden Glasses (pages 34–45)

Before you read

23 In this story someone loses a pair of glasses. Holmes studies the glasses, and then describes their owner. What information can a pair of glasses give you about their owner?

24 Write the names of these people in the story.

    a the detective   ....

    b the professor   ....

    c the gardener   ....

    d the cook   ....

    e the servant girl   ....

    f the secretary   ....

    g the murdered man   ....

25 Which is the right word?

    a Mr Smith was killed in *his bedroom / the professor's study*.

    b When Smith was murdered, the professor was *working / in bed*.

    c The pair of glasses belong to *a rich woman with weak eyes / a pretty woman with a thin nose*.

    d The mark by the keyhole in the cupboard door was made by *Mrs Hopkins / the murderer*.

    e The professor says he enjoys working and *walking / smoking*.

    f The cook says that the professor ate a *large / small* lunch that day.

After you read

26 Discuss these questions.

    a What do we know about the person who murdered Mr Smith?

    b What does Holmes discover about the cupboard in the study?

27 Work with another student. Have this conversation.

    Student A: You are Holmes. Ask the professor about his life and his work. Ask him what he knows about the murder.

    Student B: You are Professor Coram. Answer Holmes's questions.

The Golden Glasses (pages 45–50)

Before you read

28 A strange woman killed Smith. Discuss these questions.

    a Where is she now?

    b Who is she?

    c What was she looking for?

29 Are these sentences right (✓) or wrong (✗)?

    a After she murdered Smith, the woman ran out into
       the garden.   .....

    b The woman is Russian but the professor is English.   .....

    c The professor is the woman's husband.   .....

    d The woman got information and a key to the
       cupboard from Mr Smith.   .....

    e The woman took poison before she talked to Holmes.   .....

    f Holmes and Watson take Alexis's letters to the Russian
       Embassy.   .....

After you read

30 Why are these things important to the story?

    a the two passages in the house

    b the professor's breakfast and lunch

    c the ash from Holmes's cigarettes

31 Discuss these questions.

    a Was the woman a good or a bad person? Why?

    b Was the professor a good or a bad person? Why?

32 Work with another student. Have this conversation at the Russian
Embassy in London.

    Student A: You are Holmes. Give the packet of letters to the
                    person in the embassy. Answer his/her questions.

    Student B: You work in the embassy. Ask about the men who
                    have brought the letters. Then ask about the letters.
                    Are you interested in them?

Writing

33 In 'The Six Napoleons' Holmes shows that he is very intelligent.
He also has a good memory. Give some examples of his skills and
how they helped to solve this case.

34 At the end of 'The Six Napoleons', Lestrade invites Holmes to Scotland Yard to talk to other police officers at Scotland Yard about this case. Write Lestrade's speech to the officers when he introduces Holmes. He will talk about Holmes's detective work in general, then give a little information about this case.

35 Imagine you are Mr Harker, in 'The Six Napoleons'. Write an exciting story for your newspaper about the madman who hated Napoleon. You can only use the information that you were given. Some of the story is, perhaps, not true, but that doesn't matter.

36 In 'The Norwood Builder' there is no murder. Explain why it is a crime story.

37 Imagine you are McFarlane's mother in 'The Norwood Builder'. After the case, when your son is free again, you write to Sherlock Holmes. Thank him for helping your son.

38 Imagine that you are Anna before the start of 'The Golden Glasses'. Write a letter to Alexis in prison in Russia. You know where your husband is living now. You are going to try to find his letters.

39 Write about the part that Dr Watson plays in these stories. Why is he important?

40 Which of the three stories did you like best? Write about the story and why you enjoyed it.

41 Write the beginning of another Sherlock Holmes story. Who comes to his rooms? Why? What is the problem?

42 Compare Sherlock Holmes with a fictional detective from the literature of your country. How are they similar? How are they different?

Answers for the Activities in this book are available from the Penguin Readers website. A free Activity Worksheet is also available from the website. Activity Worksheets are part of the Penguin Teacher Support Programme, which also includes Progress Tests and Graded Reader Guidelines. For more information, please visit: www.penguinreaders.com.

WORD LIST

ash (n) something soft and grey that falls from a burning cigarette

bust (n) the head, shoulders and upper body of a person's body, in stone or metal

case (n) a problem that a detective or the police try to solve

embassy (n) a building in a foreign country where people do work for their own country

hang (v) to kill someone by hanging them from something around their neck

lawyer (n) a professional who has studied the law

mad (adj) ill in the head

mark (n) a small dark or dirty area on something like a shirt

motive (n) the reason for doing something

optician (n) someone who tests your eyes

passage (n) a narrow area with walls each side, between two or more rooms

pearl (n) a small, round, expensive white thing that comes from a sea animal. Women wear pearls around their necks.

print (n) a sign, like a footprint or a thumbprint, that someone has been in a place

poison (n) something that can kill people or animals. For example, there are poisons in some plants and in the bites of some animals.

professor (n) an important teacher at a university

rabbit (n) a small animal with long ears that lives in holes in the ground

revolutionary (n) someone who wants a change to a completely different kind of government

servant (n) someone who works in another person's house

wax (n) something that was put on envelopes or letters in the past. It was used to close them.

will (n) a signed written paper. It tells people who will have your money after your death.

A Scandal in Bohemia
Sir Arthur Conan Doyle

All kinds of people, from shopkeepers to kings, want the help of
Sherlock Holmes in these six stories about the adventures of the
famous detective. Who put a diamond in a chicken? Why is there
a club for men with red hair? How did the man at the lake die? Can
Sherlock Holmes solve the mysteries?

Sherlock Holmes and the Mystery of Boscombe Pool
Sir Arthur Conan Doyle

Who killed Charles McCarthy? And why? Was it really his son?
Sherlock Holmes, the brilliant detective, must answer these
questions with the help of this trusted friend, Dr Watson.

Three Adventures of Sherlock Holmes
Sir Arthur Conan Doyle

What is the mysterious 'speckled band'? Are five orange pips a
sign that someone will die soon? Is the banker's son a thief?

*There are hundreds of Penguin Readers to choose from – world classics,
film adaptations, modern-day crime and adventure, short stories,
biographies, American classics, non-fiction, plays ...*

For a complete list of all Penguin Readers titles, please contact your local
Pearson Longman office or visit our website.

The No. 1 Ladies' Detective Agency
Alexander McCall Smith

Precious Ramotswe is a kind, warm hearted and large African lady. She is also the only female private detective in Botswana. Her agency – the No. 1 Ladies' Detective Agency – is the best in the country. With the help of her secretary, Mma Makutsi, and her best friend, Mr JLB Matekoni, she solves a number of difficult – and sometimes dangerous – problems. A missing husband, a missing finger and a missing child – she will solve these mysteries in her own special way.

K's First Case
L.G. Alexander

This is a detective story with a difference. We invite *you* to help solve the case.

Katrina Kirby is a detective, and people call her 'K'. There has been a murder in a big country house. K knows that one of five people murdered Sir Michael Gray. Who did it? How? Why?

The Ring
Bernard Smith

One day Rafael was well; the next day he was completely mad. What happened to make him crazy? The story of Rafael and his gold ring is a story of murder, mystery and love. Many people know part of the story, but only Rafael knows what really happened. And Rafael is mad.

There are hundreds of Penguin Readers to choose from – world classics, film adaptations, modern-day crime and adventure, short stories, biographies, American classics, non-fiction, plays ...

For a complete list of all Penguin Readers titles, please contact your local Pearson Longman office or visit our website.

www.penguinreaders.com

Longman Dictionaries

Express yourself with confidence!

*Longman has led the way in ELT dictionaries since 1935.
We constantly talk to students and teachers around the
world to find out what they need from a learner's dictionary.*

Why choose a Longman dictionary?

Easy to understand

Longman invented the Defining Vocabulary – 2000 of the most
common words which are used to write the definitions in our
dictionaries. So Longman definitions are always clear and easy
to understand.

Real, natural English

All Longman dictionaries contain natural examples taken from
real-life that help explain the meaning of a word and show you
how to use it in context.

Avoid common mistakes

Longman dictionaries are written specially for learners, and we
make sure that you get all the help you need to avoid common
mistakes. We analyse typical learners' mistakes and include
notes on how to avoid them.

Innovative CD-ROMs

Longman are leaders in dictionary CD-ROM innovation. Did
you know that a dictionary CD-ROM includes features to help
improve your pronunciation, help you practice for exams and
improve your writing skills?

**For details of all Longman dictionaries, and to choose
the one that's right for you, visit our website:**

www.longman.com/dictionaries